TO:

_____

FROM:

_____

DATE:

_____

HOW MANY PEOPLE MAINTAIN THE HOUSE?

The Power of One

Deaconess Angeline Eshun Kesse

Written Words Publishing LLC
P.O. Box 462622
Aurora, Colorado 80046
www.writtenwordspublishing.com

Published by Written Words Publishing LLC June 17, 2024.

ISBN: 978-1-961610-15-6 (paperback)
ISBN: 978-1-961610-16-3 (hardcover)
ISBN: 978-1-961610-17-0 (eBook)

Library of Congress Control Number: 2024910793

Cover designed by Written Words Publishing LLC

Manufactured and printed in the United States of America

DEDICATION

This book is dedicated first to Jehovah El Elyon for His Indescribable Gift. Second, to my children and grandchildren. Third, to the leadership of Bethel Fellowship. Fourth, to all my spiritual sons and daughters and Bethel Fellowship members worldwide. And fifth, to everyone who wants to have more of God in their life and is ready and willing to obey the Master's call to maintain the house and make a difference.

TABLE OF CONTENTS

ACKNOWLEDGEMENTS

This work would not have been completed if it was not for the valuable input from a few people whom God brought into my life. First, I give thanks to Jehovah El Elyon, our Father, our Lord Jesus Christ, and the Holy Spirit for the revelation of this book.

I also thank Dr. Joseph Arthur-Asmah and Minister Jemima who took the Word and offered their valuable time and skills to birth this book. May the Lord reward them abundantly.

Finally, I appreciate Apostle Victor Acquah Djan for inputting his years of rich writing experience. His insight and wisdom were truly a blessing.

ENDORSEMENTS

Everyone on this planet Earth is born to make a difference. However, when we celebrate the new life we have in Christ because our heart belongs to Him, we make an impact. *How Many People Maintain the House* by Angeline Eshun Kesse is an interesting book born in its own time. It emphasizes the power of one, how God calls one person and impacts that one to make a difference. To maintain the house and make a difference requires faith that remains resolute and steadfast. For the most part, ordinary men and women from all walks of life sought God with singleness of heart and were used by God beyond human comprehension. According to the author, it does not take a multitude to maintain the house. It takes willingness of heart to contribute and maintain the house. I highly recommended the book.

Dr. Joseph Arthur-Asmah
Denver, Colorado

"Whatever you have learned or received or heard from me, or seen in me—put it into practice. And the God of peace will be with you" (Philippians 4:9 NIV).

The book, *How Many People Maintain the House* by Angeline Eshun Kesse, is a very insightful narration of how God used great men and women in biblical times to effect changes and impact the world in a tremendous way. She brought to light the various change agents in the Bible and how they availed themselves to be utilized by the Holy Spirit Himself to become beacons of change to ensure the gospel was propagated and the message of the Most High God was received in season.

As children of the Most High God, we are afforded opportunities to be change agents by leaning on the power of God to be equipped to make a difference in this world. This book emphasizes on the "power of one" and talks about the need for us, as children of God, to have a willing and obedient heart to navigate the complexities of this world to be instruments of change. We need to be courageous, obedient, faithful, determined, and, above all, have endurance for the journey.

It takes the grace of God to be endowed and empowered to stand as a person to make a difference. As you read the book, you will navigate through the experiences of life and find the secret to leaning on God to make a difference. What separates people from being successful or unsuccessful is the difference they make. This is a book to refresh and ignite your faith as an individual to make a difference. The difference you make will become the force that propels you to become a mountain mover and an icon of hope to the community. This book can transform your life to be that "one person" who maintains the house; that "one person" who makes a difference in life and leaves an indelible mark of the Lord's fingerprints behind.

Remember, this book is for you to make the difference you have always been dreaming of. I unequivocally recommend this book. It will make you a change agent for the kingdom of God. The journey starts with you as an individual.

Dr. (Rev) Yaa Amoakoa Caternor
Clarksburg, Maryland

In the book, *How Many People Maintain the House* by Angeline Eshun Kesse, we see the significant illustration of the power of one. Solomon, the wisest man who ever lived, said in Ecclesiastes 7:19 that wisdom does more for a person than ten rulers can do for a city. One person can change the course of life, one person can impact a whole nation, and an individual can make a positive impact on generations to come.

Nabal used words that stirred up anger in David (1 Samuel 25). So, David intended to slay Nabal and his servants. Abigail, in the Bible, talked with him to prevent the anger from leading to destruction. Her comforting words turned away the wrath that could have harmed the entire members in the house. The Bible says in Proverbs 15:1 that a soft word turns away wrath, but a harsh word stirs up anger. One person's encouragement can stop a

person from committing suicide. Another person's inspiration can spark a new generation of youth turning to the Lord for hope. One person's prayer of faith can stop the wrath of God and move mountains to impact many lives. Indeed, it takes just one person to maintain the house. It takes one family member, one youth, one student, one teacher, one director, one professor, one doctor to maintain the house.

As you read the book, *How Many People Maintain the House*, become that one person of influence to maintain the house. Become that one person to bring a change in the family history. Become that one person to bring the light of holiness, to reveal God's revelation through wisdom, knowledge and grace. And become that one person to make a difference in this generation. This book is to empower you to stop procrastinating and take that bold step to do something for impact. I greatly recommend this book.

Paa-Kwesi Adom Obeng
Student
Aurora, Colorado

FOREWORD

Written by Apostle Victor Acquah Djan

"For I know the plans I have for you,' declares the Lord, 'plans to prosper you and not to harm you, plans to give you hope and a future" (Jeremiah 29:11 NIV).

God told Jeremiah, "I know the thoughts I have for you, they are thoughts of good and not of evil to bring you to an expected end." God's plan gives hope and a future. His plan gives our lives a meaning. His Word is the compass that guides our journey through time, fulfilling the plans and destinations He has designed for us.

Angeline Eshun Kesse, also known as Mama Angie, through the inspiration of the Holy Spirit, has compiled from the Word of God, the compass of life and the inspiring stories of men and women who were used by God to make significant impact on Earth. The stories of these biblical characters are so dynamic and applicable to our lives today.

She highlights the state of the heart needed for God to be able to work through us and make us individuals who "maintain the house." The "house" defines the different areas of life where God can use us to be impactful such as our marriages, families, cities, states,

generations, nations, or even worldwide. It challenges us to stand up and be used by God for His glory and honor.

The virtues of availability to God, the significant importance of oneness as children of God, the commitment to understand our place as the image of God on Earth, the wholesomeness of godly wisdom, the following of God's divine strategies, and the listening to His voice at all times are greatly illustrated in this book. This piece of literature will help us learn to become usable by God. Simple to read, the pages are filled with abundant inspiring stories which will help catapult us into the greatness that God wants to establish in our lives and also through us to benefit generations not yet born.

How Many People Maintain the House is a call to stand up to our uniqueness and recognize our usability when we approach God with the right heart and allow Him to shape in us the needed character to sustain us as impact-makers in this world. Be ready to read the familiar and unfamiliar stories that God will use to inspire, strengthen, equip, and empower us to become that "one person" He will use for something great to His glory.

Be blessed!

Apostle Victor Acquah Djan
Missionary in Germany
Founder and Leader of European Missions

INTRODUCTION

"Blessed is the man that walketh not in the counsel of the ungodly, nor standeth in the way of sinners, nor sitteth in the seat of the scornful. But his delight is in the law of the LORD; *and in his law doth he meditate day and night. And he shall be like a tree planted by the rivers of water, that bringeth forth his fruit in his season; his leaf also shall not wither; and whatsoever he doeth shall prosper"* (Psalm 1:1-3).

"I have not failed the command of His lips; I have treasured the words of His mouth more than my necessary food" (Job 23:12 NASB).

"Thy words were found, and I did eat them; and thy word was unto me the joy and rejoicing of mine heart: for I am called by thy name, O LORD *God of hosts"* (Jeremiah 15:16).

Preaching, teaching and counseling God's people through the Word of God for over 30 years has been a unique gift of divine grace which has allowed me to live in the blessedness of Psalm 1:1-3, Job 23:12 and the joy of Jeremiah 15:16. The task of writing this divinely inspired book was approached with prayerfulness, humility and timeless principles from the Word of God. The goal is to bring us rest from all forms of human

1

traditions to a Christlike mindset, magnify our Lord, exalt His name above all names, and enlighten the saints to bring a difference in this dispensation. Therefore, be diligent to enter that rest. May the Holy Spirit enlighten us, so we do not discard the offer of God's rest.

How Many People Maintain the House was written with the reader in mind and calls them to make a difference as one person who maintains the house. The contents are words of knowledge and wisdom that will help one crossover the challenges of life without stumbling. It focuses on how one person could bring a difference to families, nations and generations with the direction and help of God. This book is a comfortable addition to personal libraries and also a tool to set us on a new passage towards freedom, success and making a difference by obeying the Word of God.

The Word of God is described in Hebrews 4:12 as *"quick, and powerful, and sharper than any twoedged sword, piercing even to the dividing asunder of soul and spirit, and of the joints and marrow, and is a discerner of the thoughts and intents of the heart."* He has given us His Word to penetrate the depths of who we are and transform us from the inside out. The truth in this book, through the eyes of God, will transform us from the inside out. The assessment and revelation leads, guides and directs us to understand that God does not need many people to maintain the house.

- A house is a building for human or animal habitation. But in the context of this book, a house

represents a family, church, city, nation, generation, group of people, and many more.

- "Maintain" is being used to express "making a difference or an impact."
- So, to "maintain the house" will mean making a difference or an impact in a family, church, city, nation, generation, group of people, and many more.

In 2 Timothy 3:16-17, we see that we will be equipped for every good work with the understanding of the number of people needed to maintain the house. Psalm 119:105 also tells us that God's Word is a light that illuminates our way forward. However, it is up to us to align ourselves with the message to light our path. The Word of God is light for our path and health for our flesh. It is the revealed will of God for our lives.

Truth is not in the eye of the beholder, but truth is based on the Word of God. However, our perception of what is happening in our lives affects our faith which then determines how we respond in situations. God is asking us, would we like to make a difference in our home, in our generation? What do we want to do with our life? Get the vision of making a difference. Deal with our fear and allow Him to guide us each step of the way to make a difference in His Kingdom. Stop making excuses. God has a plan for us, just ask Him to show us so we can start making a difference in our home. God wants our availability. When God puts a thirsting in our soul, we will have a different attitude. The hunger for Him will change us.

Matthew 5:6 says, *"Blessed are they which do hunger and thirst after righteousness: for they shall be filled."* As we learn to hear the voice of God, we will notice that He speaks in a variety of ways. He is not limited to any particular method or style. Sometimes, He speaks through godly men and women. Other times, He speaks through circumstances. Occasionally, He speaks directly to our spirit. We must hear the Word of God with our heart so we can maintain the home and make an impact.

CHAPTER ONE

MAKING A DIFFERENCE

Proverbs 6:16-19 teaches us there are seven things the Lord hates. To make a difference, we must avoid a proud look, a lying tongue, hands that shed innocent blood, a heart that devises wicked imaginations, feet that are swift in running to mischief, a false witness that speaks lies, and he that sows discord among brethren.

2 Timothy 3:1-5 (NIV) says, *"But mark this: There will be terrible times in the last days. People will be lovers of themselves, lovers of money, boastful, proud, abusive, disobedient to their parents, ungrateful, unholy, without love, unforgiving, slanderous, without self-control, brutal, not lovers of the good, treacherous, rash, conceited, lovers of pleasure rather than lovers of God—having a form of godliness but denying its power. Have nothing to do with such people."*

God is looking for character, not talent. A person who makes a difference commits to be closer to God every day. They are disciplined and diligent. They have a sense of adventure and handle obstacles differently than the masses. They can be compared to a tree planted by the rivers of water whose will is surrendered to God. Like a weaned child, they are calm and peaceful. They should be a person of character who walks and operates in love. A person who makes a difference will be transformed from an ordinary person to an extraordinary person. Be blessed today to make a difference!

In Scripture we can find a lot of individuals who yielded themselves to God and made a significant difference in their generation and beyond. We can consider a few in this book to challenge us to stand up and make a difference.

A. Jesus Made a Difference

The Lion of the Tribe of Judah

The Earth was given to man to manage and have dominion over it. Through sin, man lost control to Satan. It needed to be redeemed and restored back to man. A failure to find a redeemer means the Sovereignty of God's Earth will forever remain in the hands of Satan. Jesus, the Lion of the tribe of Judah, willingly took the sealed scroll, which was the title deed to this Earth. The deed was sealed to prevent unauthorized opening since it is a very important legal document about the ownership of the Earth. The seals are the first seven series of divine judgment out of the scroll poured out on Earth in rapid succession during the great tribulation. The seals certify and guarantee the authenticity of the document. Only a legally qualified person could take such a scroll and open it to reveal its content. The qualified person must be sinless and truly righteous.

The question arose in Heaven, who is worthy to redeem and rescue the Earth? Who has the ability and right to break the seals and open the scroll? No one except Jesus, the King of Kings and the Lord of Lords, was willing and qualified to break the seals. The breaking of each seal released judgment on Earth, but He alone could take all our judgments upon Himself to redeem us back to God.

Let us read this redemption story from Revelation 5:1-14 (NLT):

"Then I saw a scroll in the right hand of the one who was sitting on the throne. There was writing on the inside and the outside of the scroll, and it was sealed with seven seals. And I saw a strong angel, who shouted with a loud voice: 'Who is worthy to break the seals on this scroll and open it?' But no one in heaven or on earth or under the earth was able to open the scroll and read it. "Then I began to weep bitterly because no one was found worthy to open the scroll and read it. But one of the twenty-four elders said to me, 'Stop weeping! Look, the Lion of the tribe of Judah, the heir to David's throne, has won the victory. He is worthy to open the scroll and its seven seals.' Then I saw a Lamb that looked as if it had been slaughtered, but it was now standing between the throne and the four living beings and among the twenty-four elders. He had seven horns and seven eyes, which represent the sevenfold Spirit of God that is sent out into every part of the earth. He stepped forward and took the scroll from the right hand of the one sitting on the throne. And when he took the scroll, the four living beings and the

twenty-four elders fell down before the Lamb. Each one had a harp, and they held gold bowls filled with incense, which are the prayers of God's people. And they sang a new song with these words: 'You are worthy to take the scroll and break its seals and open it. For you were slaughtered, and your blood has ransomed people for God from every tribe and language and people and nation. And you have caused them to become a Kingdom of priests for our God. And they will reign on the earth.' Then I looked again, and I heard the voices of thousands and millions of angels around the throne and of the living beings and the elders. And they sang in a mighty chorus: 'Worthy is the Lamb who was slaughtered—to receive power and riches and wisdom and strength and honor and glory and blessing.' And then I heard every creature in heaven and on earth and under the earth and in the sea. They sang: 'Blessing and honor and glory and power belong to the one sitting on the throne and to the Lamb forever and ever.' And the four living beings said, 'Amen!' And the twenty-four elders fell down and worshiped the Lamb."

The Lamb Said, "Send Me"

When God wanted to bring mankind back to Himself, there was a meeting in Heaven and only one person shouted out, "Send Me and I will go." The Lamb gave His own life. He emptied Himself and became a servant to all. The worthiness of the Lamb who was slain reminds us God came to our level. The Lamb made Himself nothing. He was willing to give up everything for our sustenance. So, it takes one person to make a difference and say, "Yes, I will go."

In Revelations 5, we were told that only the Lamb is worthy to take the scroll, break its seals and open it. When He was crucified, His blood paid the ransom for every tribe, language, people, and nation. He is the only one who made a difference by coming down to bring mankind back. He is the only one who stood up and said, "Yes."

After He opened the seal and came to redeem mankind, mankind became disobedient, very doubtful and many stopped trusting God. As children of God, we must trust His Word. We must see with the eyes of the Spirit and hear with our heart. Doing so will give us the ability to be the one who makes a difference in our time and generation. Even though many will come to help, only one needs to step forward to make a difference.

B. Isaiah Made a Difference

Isaiah's Willingness

When the Lord needed someone to warn the people to call them to repentance, Isaiah offered willingly to be that person. The Bible says in Isaiah 6:8-13 (NLT):

"Then I heard the Lord asking, 'Whom should I send as a messenger to this people? Who will go for us?' I said, 'Here I am. Send me.' And he said, 'Yes, go, and say to this people, 'Listen carefully, but do not understand. Watch closely but learn nothing.' Harden the hearts of these people.

9

Plug their ears and shut their eyes. That way, they will not see with their eyes, nor hear with their ears, nor understand with their hearts and turn to me for healing.' Then I said, 'Lord, how long will this go on?' And he replied, 'Until their towns are empty, their houses are deserted, and the whole country is a wasteland; until the LORD has sent everyone away, and the entire land of Israel lies deserted. If even a tenth—a remnant—survive, it will be invaded again and burned. But as a terebinth or oak tree leaves a stump when it is cut down, so Israel's stump will be a holy seed."

Isaiah's response, "Here I am. Send me," also highlights this point that God calls but one. Isaiah's answer was an immediate, unwavering decision. God does not need help, for He is a God who could do everything alone. Yet, He desires to involve His people. It is a privilege to do God's will. It is a privilege to be included in His plans. It is a privilege to make a difference in His vineyard. God posed a question and Isaiah responded. Through this, we can see God's nature and His attributes. God speaks and interacts with His people. God was looking for a willing heart to make a difference and Isaiah was obedient to His call. Isaiah is a model of a child of God who kept persevering to make an impact. Are you ready to make a difference? So, how many people maintain the house? It took one person, Isaiah, to stand and make a difference.

C. Abraham Made a Difference

Abraham's Willingness

When God was bringing Abraham away from his family, He focused on only one person. The Bible says in Genesis 12:1, *"Now the LORD had said unto Abram, Get thee out of the country, and from thy kindred, and from thy father's house, unto a land that I will shew thee."* In Genesis 17:5, when he was 99 years old, God changed Abram's name to Abraham. When God called Abraham from Ur in Mesopotamia, he did not question God but obeyed. He was to travel to undesignated land that he was shown later. God told him that He would bless him and his descendants and through him all families of the earth, including yours and mine, would be blessed. Generation increases come and go, but God's promise to Abraham stands. Can you imagine God telling you that you will one day own a whole country? The Bible says God watches over His Word to perform it. Abraham courageously had to leave. God called but one and now we all partake of the blessings of Abraham's obedience and greatness.

As humans, depending on the situation we are going through, we sometimes doubt. The Bible says hope deferred makes the heart sick. Abraham was a little doubtful and God said, "I will send your descendant into slavery for four hundred years." And the Lord will remember the covenant he made with Abraham. God never forgets His covenants with men.

Are we willing to make a difference? God is waiting for our availability to make an impact in our home. The Word of God says we must run with perseverance the race that is set before us. Everyone has their own race to run and we must move in God's direction. He calls us individually and all we must do is to submit to the work of the Holy Ghost and move when Jesus says move. So, how many people maintain the house? Every indication shows God calls but one person to make the impact. As we are called, He gives us helpers, but it takes one person to honor the call and rise above their circumstances to obey the call to maintain their home. We must come out of our comfort zone, and when we do, we will look at the problems we face from our position in Jesus. When we get out of our comfort zone to impact and make a difference, God will get hold of us, and suddenly, we will connect with the Holy Spirit. Under His leadership, we will be making a difference. We will be able to maintain the house by grace.

Oneness Attracts Divine Intervention

God Restrained Abimelech

In Genesis 20:1-18 (NLT), the Bible says:

"Abraham moved south to the Negev and lived for a while between Kadesh and Shur, and then he moved on to Gerar. While living there as a foreigner, Abraham introduced his wife, Sarah, by saying, 'She is my sister.' So King Abimelech of Gerar sent for Sarah and had her brought to

him at his palace. But that night God came to Abimelech in a dream and told him, 'You are a dead man, for that woman you have taken is already married!' But Abimelech had not slept with her yet, so he said, 'Lord, will you destroy an innocent nation? Didn't Abraham tell me, 'She is my sister'? And she herself said, 'Yes, he is my brother.' I acted in complete innocence! My hands are clean.' In the dream God responded, 'Yes, I know you are innocent. That's why I kept you from sinning against me, and why I did not let you touch her. Now return the woman to her husband, and he will pray for you, for he is a prophet. Then you will live. But if you don't return her to him, you can be sure that you and all your people will die.' Abimelech got up early the next morning and quickly called all his servants together. When he told them what had happened, his men were terrified. Then Abimelech called for Abraham. 'What have you done to us?' he demanded. 'What crime have I committed that deserves treatment like this, making me and my kingdom guilty of this great sin? No one should ever do what you have done! Whatever possessed you to do such a thing?' Abraham replied, 'I thought, 'This is a godless place. They will want my wife and will kill me to get her.' And she really is my sister, for we both have the same father, but different mothers. And I married her. When God called me to leave my father's home and to travel from place to place, I told her, 'Do me a favor. Wherever we go, tell the people that I am your brother.' Then Abimelech took some of his sheep and goats, cattle, and male and female servants, and he presented them to Abraham. He also returned his wife, Sarah, to him. Then Abimelech said, 'Look over my land and choose any place where you would like to live.' And he said to Sarah, 'Look, I am giving your 'brother' 1,000 pieces of silver in the presence of all these witnesses. This is to compensate you for any wrong I may have done to you. This will settle any claim against me, and your reputation is cleared.' Then Abraham prayed to God, and God healed Abimelech, his wife, and his female servants, so they could have children. For the LORD had caused all the women to be infertile because of what happened with Abraham's wife, Sarah."

Abraham perceived that the people in Abimelech's country were not godly and did not fear God, so he chose to present Sarah as his sister. If Sarah and Abraham were not one, they would not have gotten what they were given. This is not to justify the lie they told but to highlight their oneness as a couple. Because they were one, whatever they needed, they received.

God moves with people who have a common faith and understanding. He will not move with people who do not believe in Him. It takes only one person to come to the point of understanding "oneness" for things to change. Things can change in a marriage when there is a spiritual understanding that "my spouse and I are one."

Couples need to focus and decide to build a relationship of oneness that will make a greater impact, instead of focusing their attention on property acquisition and other material things which are temporal. Some spouses even acquire properties without the knowledge of their partner. Properties are good but we must prioritize the relationship to each other. The fight for temporal things leads often to tensions at home, financial pressures and deep misunderstandings which can break the home apart if care is not taken.

We need love for each other and the spirit of knowledge, wisdom, and discernment to build healthy relationships with eternal value before God. It is not easy and we cannot do it all alone. It takes "oneness" with God to manage the house. We need to help our generation to learn, understand and believe this truth.

D. Moses Made a Difference

Moses and the Burning Bush

God sought for one person, a man called Moses, in Exodus 3:1-10 (NIV):

"Now Moses was tending the flock of Jethro his father-in-law, the priest of Midian, and he led the flock to the far side of the wilderness and came to Horeb, the mountain of God. There the angel of the LORD appeared to him in flames of fire from within a bush. Moses saw that though the bush was on fire it did not burn up. So Moses thought, 'I will go over and see this strange sight—why the bush does not burn up.' When the LORD saw that he had gone over to look, God called to him from within the bush, 'Moses! Moses!' And Moses said, 'Here I am.' 'Do not come any closer,' God said. 'Take off your sandals, for the place where you are standing is holy ground.' Then he said, 'I am the God

of your father, the God of Abraham, the God of Isaac and the God of Jacob.' At this, Moses hid his face, because he was afraid to look at God. The LORD said, 'I have indeed seen the misery of my people in Egypt. I have heard them crying out because of their slave drivers, and I am concerned about their suffering. So I have come down to rescue them from the hand of the Egyptians and to bring them up out of that land into a good and spacious land, a land flowing with milk and honey—the home of the Canaanites, Hittites, Amorites, Perizzites, Hivites and Jebusites. And now the cry of the Israelites has reached me, and I have seen the way the Egyptians are oppressing them. So now, go. I am sending you to Pharaoh to bring my people the Israelites out of Egypt."

God calls each one individually. When Moses heard God call his name, he responded. Only one person has to turn and see the glory of God. One person can make a difference in the household, in the family, in the generation. It is only one person who must turn their mind and position themself to bring a difference. It does not take two, from creation up till today.

E. Mankind Makes a Difference

Mankind is Created in the Image of God

In Genesis 1:27-28 (NIV), the Bible says:

"So God created mankind in his own image, in the image of God he created them; male and female he created them.

God blessed them and said to them, 'Be fruitful and increase in number; fill the earth and subdue it. Rule over the fish in the sea and the birds in the sky and over every living creature that moves on the ground.'"

It is also written in Genesis 2:7,18-25 (NIV):

"Then the LORD God formed a man from the dust of the ground and breathed into his nostrils the breath of life, and the man became a living being...The LORD God said, 'It is not good for the man to be alone. I will make a helper suitable for him.' Now the LORD God had formed out of the ground all the wild animals and all the birds in the sky. He brought them to the man to see what he would name them; and whatever the man called each living creature, that was its name. So the man gave names to all the livestock, the birds in the sky and all the wild animals. But for Adam no suitable helper was found. So the LORD God caused the man to fall into a deep sleep; and while he was sleeping, he took one of the man's ribs and then closed up the place with flesh. Then the LORD God made a woman from the rib he had taken out of the man, and he brought her to the man. The man said, 'This is now bone of my bones and flesh of my flesh; she shall be called 'woman,' for she was taken out of man.' That is why a man leaves his father and mother and is united to his wife, and they become one flesh. Adam and his wife were both naked, and they felt no shame."

God, Himself, said, "Let Me create man in My own image and My likeness," and He created Adam, one person. Then, the Lord said that it is not good for him to be alone, so He took the rib of Adam and created a woman. We can say that there is no difference between Eve and Adam, they are the same. They are one because God did not take another image, but used the same Adam. God took his rib to create Eve. However, God added something extra for her to function. She is called woman because of God's extra addition. When the word "wo" is separated from woman, it is "man." The "wo" represents the womb. So, in effect, God did not create two people. God created only one person and from the one, He started the process of multiplying man on earth.

Isaiah 30:17 (NKJV) says, *"One thousand shall flee at the threat of one, At the threat of five you shall flee, Till you are left as a pole on top of a mountain And as a banner on a hill."* Also, Deuteronomy 32:30 (NLT) says, *"How could one person chase a thousand of them, and two people put ten thousand to flight, unless their Rock had sold them, unless the LORD had given them up?"* The Bible also says in Ecclesiastes 4:9 (NLT), *"Two people are better off than one, for they can help each other succeed."* In Genesis 2:24 (NLT), it is written, *"…the two are united into one."*

Thinking that when there are two, then something can be achieved or accomplished, is incorrect. The Scriptures make it clear that God starts His processes with one person. When He gets more people involved, they must work together in unity. An example is, God used one person, like David, to defeat Goliath. Then, the army of Israel joined him to fight the rest of the fleeing army that came with Goliath. God worked with a team, the army of Israel, but the victory process started with one person, David. This emphasizes the need to come into a common understanding that we are one. It shows that if someone has an idea and another person has a different idea, they should come together as one, then they can achieve more. So, oneness ultimately causes two people to have a common understanding. It does not matter where they come from or whether they are educated or not. If they are together, they should be one.

This oneness also points to having one common faith, i.e., believing the same God. It is not a believer and non-believer being one. If one of the individuals does not know Christ, does not have the mind of Christ or does not believe Christ, together they cannot be one.

F. Trinity Makes the Difference

Trinity – One God

The Person of the Trinity is distinct and yet fully God. The Trinity does not divide God into three parts. The Bible makes it clear that all three Persons are each one hundred percent God. The Father, Son and the Holy Spirit are all fully God. The Bible says in Isaiah 45:21 (NASB), *"...there is no other God besides Me, A righteous God and a Savior; There is none except Me."* We pray to the Father through the Son and in the Holy Spirit. God is one, in essence, three in Person.

It takes Him alone to be the Creator, the Savior and the King of Kings in the future we await—they are not three, but they are one. We do not have a different Creator, a different Savior and a different King of Kings—they refer to the one God. So, we see that it takes the one God to be always all things for us all and in all places. This is the God who makes the difference and maintains this world by the Word of His power (Hebrew 1:3). He is the perfect answer to the question: how many people maintain the house? It takes one person to maintain the house. Amen.

G. Jeremiah Makes a Difference

Jeremiah's Willingness No Matter the Personal Cost

Jeremiah served as a prophet during the last years of the Southern Kingdom, Judah, in 640-586 B.C. He was the son of Hilkiah, a Benjamite (Jeremiah 1:1) and became a prophet in the period of Judah's disobedience against God. They worshipped other gods, killed and sacrificed their sons as burnt offering unto Baal, and turned the valley of Hinnom into a valley of slaughter (Jeremiah 19). Judah also broke God's covenant by not releasing Hebrew slaves after six years of service (Jeremiah 34). Most of the prophets and priests in Jeremiah's day were not of God (Jeremiah 23). King Jehoiakim had also burnt the scroll (the Bible of their time). When Jeremiah preached against these evils, he was put in prison (Jeremiah 20). He faced the threat of death (Jeremiah 26:8), was jailed the second time (Jeremiah 37) and ended up in a dungeon. He was led with cords down below where there was no water and no food, but mire (Jeremiah 38:1-6). He even compared himself to Job (Job 3:3; Jeremiah 15:10, 20:14). God was so angry that He cast Judah out of His sight (Jeremiah 15:1-2). It was under these difficult circumstances that Jeremiah lived and preached repentance and warnings without fear of what would happen to him.

It takes one who is totally resigned to God's service to do what he did. Jeremiah yielded to God and His instructions regardless of the consequences. Taking a stand for the truth of the Bible could be very costly in our day and time but it is nothing compared to what Jeremiah had to fearlessly and boldly endure. He was one man availing himself to be used by God to correct His people and lead them back to the right path. He distinguished himself for God's use in a very corrupt, rebellious and decaying society. He sought God, not human commendation. Such are the characteristics of Jeremiah. He falls into the ranks of one who does not only build the house but maintains the house for God's glory.

Just as Jeremiah endured much for the sake of God's Word entrusted unto him to proclaim, we are also called to stand up against the corruption in our own societies and proclaim the truths of the Gospel of Jesus Christ. There will be opposition and many persecutions, but no matter what, remember that Jesus said, *"be of good cheer, I have overcome the world"* (John 16:33 NKJV). Will you be the one?

H. Elijah Makes a Difference

Elijah's Willingness to Take Risk for God

Elijah lived and proclaimed God's Word during the period of extreme wickedness, under Ahab, the seventh king of Israel (2 Chronicles 18). During this period, idolatrous worship of Baal, along with loose, immoral, sensual, lustful orgies of goddess Ashtoreth, had been introduced in Israel by Queen Jezebel. Persecution of God's true prophets was also common (1 Kings 18). Because of Israel's wickedness, Elijah pronounced drought upon Israel for three and a half years. He contested with the prophets of Baal, won the contest, and killed four hundred and fifty of Baal's prophets. He raised a widow's dead son to life and was taken to Heaven with a chariot of fire without dying physically (2 Kings 2:11). The prophet appeared to Jesus at the Mount of Transfiguration (Mark 9:4-5) and the New Testament testified that Elijah was a man just like one of us but prayed fervently and impacted his world greatly (James 5:17-18).

Elijah's life demonstrates selflessness, bold and risk-taking faith, sensitivity to God, and the impact of prayer among others. He trusted God totally when he contested with 450 Baal prophets. He was of fearless spirit and sought God and His approval alone. He always stood for

God so God made him stand out in the crowd as "one" who could maintain the house.

Being like Elijah means being bold and fearless in our convictions. It is forfeiting human praises to honor God no matter the cost. It is being men and women of repute and pursuing the mark of distinction from God. Such a one like Elijah is the one needed, not only to build, but to maintain the house for the Lord. Be one of such distinction like Elijah.

CHAPTER TWO

THE IMPACT MAKER'S LIFE

A. An Impact Maker:
Jehosheba, King Jehoram's Daughter

The Bible says in 2 Chronicles 22:10-12 (NIV), *"When Athaliah the mother of Ahaziah saw that her son was dead, she proceeded to destroy the whole royal family of the house of Judah. But Jehosheba, the daughter of King Jehoram, took Joash son of Ahaziah and stole him away from among the royal princes who were about to be murdered and put him and his nurse in a bedroom. Because Jehosheba, the daughter of King Jehoram and wife of the priest Jehoiada, was Ahaziah's sister, she hid the child from Athaliah so she could not kill him. He remained hidden with them at the temple of God for six years while Athaliah ruled the land."*

Jehosheba, the daughter of King Jehoram, took Joash, the son of Ahaziah, and hid him away from those who were going to kill him. Jehosheba, as an individual, executed a good work by wisdom to preserve the lineage of David as spoken by God. He became an impact-maker for the glory of God. That single decision ensured that there would be a continuous lineage of royals sitting on the throne of David.

Never take for granted the opportunities and the promptings of the Holy Spirit to step out in faith for Him to save a life today. We never know what the Lord will do with that one life for eternity. Decide to be an impact-maker.

B. An Impact Maker:
Priest Jehoiada, a Strategist

The Bible says in 2 Chronicles 23:1-16 (MSG):

"In the seventh year the priest Jehoiada decided to make his move and worked out a strategy with certain influential officers in the army. He picked Azariah son of Jeroham, Ishmael son of Jehohanan, Azariah son of Obed, Maaseiah son of Adaiah, and Elishaphat son of Zichri as his associates. They dispersed throughout Judah and called in the Levites from all the towns in Judah along with the heads of families. They met in Jerusalem. The gathering met in The Temple of God. They made a covenant there in The Temple. The priest Jehoiada showed them the young prince and addressed them: 'Here he is—the son of the king. He is going to rule just as GOD promised regarding the sons of David. Now this is what you must do: A third of you priests and Levites who come on duty on the Sabbath are to be posted as security guards at the gates; another third will guard the palace; and the other third will guard the foundation gate. All the people will gather in the courtyards of The Temple of GOD. No one may enter The Temple of GOD except the priests and designated Levites—they are permitted in because they've been consecrated, but all the people must do the work assigned them. The Levites are to

form a ring around the young king, weapons at the ready. Kill anyone who tries to break through your ranks. Your job is to stay with the king at all times and places, coming and going.' All the Levites and officers obeyed the orders of Jehoiada the priest. Each took charge of his men, both those who came on duty on the Sabbath and those who went off duty on the Sabbath, for Jehoiada the priest hadn't exempted any of them from duty. Then the priest armed the officers with spears and the large and small shields originally belonging to King David that were stored in The Temple of God. Well-armed, the guards took up their assigned positions for protecting the king, from one end of The Temple to the other, surrounding both Altar and Temple. Then the priest brought the prince into view, crowned him, handed him the scroll of God's covenant, and made him king. As Jehoiada and his sons anointed him they shouted, 'Long live the king!' Athaliah, hearing all the commotion, the people running around and praising the king, came to The Temple to see what was going on. Astonished, she saw the young king standing at the entrance flanked by the captains and heralds, with everybody beside themselves with joy, trumpets blaring, the choir and orchestra leading the praise. Athaliah ripped her robes in dismay and shouted, 'Treason! Treason!' Jehoiada the priest ordered the military officers, 'Drag her outside—and kill anyone who tries to follow her!' (The priest had said, 'Don't kill her inside The Temple of GOD.') So they dragged her out to the palace's horse corral and there they killed her. Jehoiada now made a *covenant between himself and the king and the people: they were to be the GOD's special people."*

Jehoiada impacted in a positive way by making his move and working out a strategy with certain influential officers in the army. His strategy included gathering in the Temple of God and making a covenant there. It is very important in our own lives to follow God's divine strategy in every situation. We all need a strategy to get us out of some stagnancy or unforeseen battles in life. We need a God inspired plan and boldness to step out of fear and limitations in our lives. I pray that God will prompt a divine strategy or ideas in you right now to become a channel of His impact on Earth. Amen.

For Reflection: A Background to Jehoiada's Story

Without the strategy, the enemy's intention was to destroy the lineage of David. But God had declared to David, *"But My mercy shall not depart from him, as I took it from Saul, whom I removed from before you. And your house and your kingdom shall be established forever before you. Your throne shall be established forever"* (2 Samuel 7:15,16 NKJV). The Lord promised David that his house would be established forever but God's promise was conditional.

The blessings to David's house were dependent on the descendant's faithfulness to the Lord. The Lord promised David's son, *"Now if you walk before Me as your father David walked, in integrity of heart and in uprightness, to do according to all that I have commanded you, and if you keep My statutes and My judgments, then I will establish the throne of your kingdom over Israel forever, as I promised David your father, saying, 'You shall not fail to have a man on the throne of Israel'"* (1 Kings 9:4-5 NKJV).

Athaliah, the Wicked Murderer

Athaliah stepped out in a negative way. She intended to destroy the whole royal family of the house of Judah. Because of God's promise to establish David's throne forever, God found a way to hide Joash and preserved him from death. This was done to fulfill God's promise to David. So, what we read about Jehoiada, the Priest, stepping out with a strategy is a continuation of God's rescue plan because of His faithfulness to His Word concerning David. The wicked Athaliah attempted to destroy the lineage but God inspired a strategy through one man for protection.

Athaliah's mother is Jezebel and her father is Ahab, so we can see where this wickedness came from. Jezebel killed the prophets of God (1 Kings 18:13). Athaliah killed the royal family—the sons, heirs to the throne of the house of Judah. She had access because she married Jehoshaphat's son and heir of the House of Judah.

The Importance of Strategy

In 1 Kings 18:13 (NKJV), Obadiah said this to Elijah: *"Was it not reported to my lord what I did when Jezebel killed the prophets of the LORD, how I hid one hundred men of the LORD's prophets, fifty to a cave, and fed them with bread and water?"*

Obadiah and the other individuals who made an impact had strategy. My question for you is: do you have a strategy from God for life?

Also, 2 Chronicles 23:9-10 tells us that the priest strategized by arming the officers with spears and shields so they could protect the king from one end of the Temple to the other. Today, we do not fight with physical weapons because we do not fight against flesh and blood. So, the weapons of our warfare are not carnal, but they are mighty through God to the pulling down of strongholds, casting down imaginations and every high thing that exalts itself against the knowledge of God. We, therefore, have the armor of God as listed in Ephesians 6:13-18 and our offensive weapon of attack is the WORD OF GOD. So, be an active student of the Word of God.

Remember that God is watching over His Word concerning our lives and families to fulfill it. He is the promise maker and the covenant keeper. We must not fear the weapons of destruction formed against us because they shall not prosper in Jesus' Name. Amen. A thousand will fall on our side and ten thousand at our right side and with our eyes, we will see the reward of the wicked, but they shall not come near us. Hallelujah!

C. An Impact Maker:
The Prophet Oded, a Good Samaritan

It is written in 2 Chronicles 28:1-8 (NIV):

"Ahaz was twenty years old when he became king, and he reigned in Jerusalem sixteen years. Unlike David his father, he did not do what was right in the eyes of the LORD. He followed the ways of the kings of Israel and also made idols for worshiping the Baals. He burned sacrifices in the Valley of Ben Hinnom and sacrificed his children in the fire, engaging in the detestable practices of the nations the LORD had driven out before the Israelites. He offered sacrifices and burned incense at the high places, on the hilltops and under every spreading tree. Therefore the LORD his God delivered him into the hands of the king of Aram. The Arameans defeated him and took many of his people as prisoners and brought them to Damascus. He was also given into the hands of the king of Israel, who inflicted heavy casualties on him. In one day Pekah son of Remaliah killed a hundred and twenty thousand soldiers in Judah—because Judah had forsaken the LORD, the God of their ancestors. Zikri, an Ephraimite warrior, killed Maaseiah the king's son, Azrikam the officer in charge of the palace, and Elkanah, second to the king. The men of Israel took captive from their fellow Israelites who were from Judah two hundred thousand wives, sons and daughters. They also took a great deal of plunder, which they carried back to Samaria."

I believe by grace—the people of Judah cried to God for mercy—they were lamenting in their heart for God to show them mercy. In their spirit, I could hear them singing, "For His mercies shall endure, ever faithful ever sure. 2 Chronicles 28:9-15 (NIV) says:

"But a prophet of the LORD *named Oded was there, and he went out to meet the army when it returned to Samaria. He said to them, 'Because the* LORD*, the God of your ancestors, was angry with Judah, he gave them into your hand. But you have slaughtered them in a rage that reaches to heaven. And now you intend to make the men and women of Judah and Jerusalem your slaves. But aren't you also guilty of sins against the* LORD *your God? Now listen to me! Send back your fellow Israelites you have taken as prisoners, for the* LORD*'s fierce anger rests on you.' Then some of the leaders in Ephraim—Azariah son of Jehohanan, Berekiah son of Meshillemoth, Jehizkiah son of Shallum, and Amasa son of Hadlai—confronted those who were arriving from the war. 'You must not bring those prisoners here,' they said, 'or we will be guilty before the* LORD*. Do you intend to add to our sin and guilt? For our guilt is already great, and his fierce anger rests on Israel.' So the soldiers gave up the prisoners and plunder in the presence of the officials and all the assembly. The men designated by name took the prisoners, and from the plunder they clothed all who were naked. They provided them with clothes and sandals, food and drink, and healing balm. All those who were weak they put on donkeys. So they took them back to their fellow Israelites at Jericho, the City of Palms, and returned to Samaria."*

Now, who is Prophet Oded? Oded's son is Azariah the prophet who met King Asa. King Asa was Jehoshaphat's father. The Bible says in 2 Chronicles 15:1-2, *"And the Spirit of God came upon Azariah the son of Oded:*

And he went out to meet Asa, and said unto him, Hear ye me, Asa, and all Judah and Benjamin; The LORD is with you, while ye be with him; and if ye seek him, he will be found of you; but if ye forsake him, he will forsake you."

In this story, we see that Oded stepped in to become a good Samaritan to the people of Judah. The Bible says Oded, the Prophet of God, was from Samaria and met the army of Israel who were returning with captives from Judah. He urged the army to return the people of Judah which they had made their slaves.

The slaves could have been treated badly: they could be naked, put to shame and reproach, beaten, harassed, oppressed, and even imprisoned. Whenever we are dealing with anything that makes us feel captured, imprisoned, limited, worthless, devalued, beaten, shamed or whatever, we must be ready to put on our dancing shoes because our divine intervention is on the way through one man, right now. Amen!

This Prophet Oded did not keep quiet. He did not say, "Well, it's none of my business. This is Judah and Israel fighting." He intervened with the Word and urged them to return the slaves. Now, because Prophet Oded stepped in, some of the leaders of Israel in one accord joined in this intervention and it was a success.

The people of Judah would have been slaves had the Prophet Oded not intervened. Imagine what would have happened.

For Reflection: A Background to Obed's Story

Sometimes, after God has warned us several times and we don't listen, He humbles us. In 2 Chronicles 28:19 (NIV), *"The LORD had humbled Judah because of Ahaz king of Israel, for he had promoted wickedness in Judah and had been most unfaithful to the LORD."* So, their disobedience to God landed them into this trouble but it took that same God's intervention through Prophet Oded to give them another chance to be free from slavery. This action of God towards Judah is called grace. They could not earn it so the God of mercy helped them. May the Lord mercifully, according to the act of grace, help us too, no matter the mistakes we have made before. Amen.

We know that man is wicked as it's exemplified throughout the Scriptures. The Bible tells us that, in one day, Pekah killed 120,000 soldiers. Because the Lord was angry with Judah, He allowed it (2 Chronicles 28:6,9). Even God Himself, when He was punishing David, killed 70,000 men in one day (2 Samuel 24:15), but Pekah wickedly killed in a rage that reached to Heaven. Let's review the example of David's punishment for a comparison.

A Comparison: David and God's Mercy

David took a census—he counted the number of people and God was displeased. It is written in 1 Chronicles 21:1-18 (GNT):

"Satan wanted to bring trouble on the people of Israel, so he made David decide to take a census. David gave orders to Joab and the other officers, 'Go through Israel, from one end of the country to the other, and count the people. I want to know how many there are.' Joab answered, 'May the LORD make the people of Israel a hundred times more numerous than they are now! Your Majesty, they are all your servants. Why do you want to do this and make the whole nation guilty?' But the king made Joab obey the order. Joab went out, traveled through the whole country of Israel, and then returned to Jerusalem. He reported to King David the total number of men capable of military service: 1,100,000 in Israel and 470,000 in Judah. Because Joab disapproved of the king's command, he did not take any census of the tribes of Levi and Benjamin. God was displeased with what had been done, so he punished Israel. David said to God, 'I have committed a terrible sin in doing this! Please forgive me. I have acted foolishly.' Then the LORD said to Gad, David's prophet, 'Go and tell David that I am giving him three choices. I will do whichever he chooses.' Gad went to David, told him what the LORD had said, and asked, 'Which is it to be? Three years of famine? Or three months of running away from the armies of your enemies? Or three days during which the LORD attacks you with his sword and sends an epidemic on your land, using his angel to bring death throughout Israel? What answer shall I give the LORD?' David replied to Gad, 'I am in a desperate situation! But I don't want to be punished by people. Let the LORD himself be the one to punish me,

because he is merciful.' So the LORD *sent an epidemic on the people of Israel, and seventy thousand of them died. Then he sent an angel to destroy Jerusalem, but he changed his mind and said to the angel, 'Stop! That's enough!' The angel was standing by the threshing place of Araunah, a Jebusite. David saw the angel standing in midair, holding his sword in his hand, ready to destroy Jerusalem. Then David and the leaders of the people—all of whom were wearing sackcloth—bowed low, with their faces touching the ground. David prayed, 'O God, I am the one who did wrong. I am the one who ordered the census. What have these poor people done?* LORD, *my God, punish me and my family, and spare your people.'"*

The number of deaths involved in the two stories clearly show us that God is merciful because He is love. Man, however, does not show any mercy; man is wicked in nature.

God used prophet Oded, as a good Samaritan, to step in to intervene and restrain the people of Israel from causing more harm to the people of Judah. Once again, God needed one available man to make such an impact and deliver Judah from slavery. Hallelujah! May you become the one person God uses to deliver a nation wherever you find yourself. Amen.

D. An Impact Maker:
The Queen Esther, Wife of King Ahasuerus

Haman's Schemes vs. Esther's Influence!

Esther, with the Hebrew name Hadassah, was chosen by King Ahasuerus or Xerxes as his queen to replace Vashti. This happened at a critical time for the Jews in the kingdom because Haman, a high official of the kingdom, was not bowed to by Mordecai, a Jew, and a low-level official of the kingdom. Therefore, Haman sought to kill him and annihilate the entire Jewish population.

Haman manipulated to secure the king's approval to execute his hatched plans. He was ready to pay ten thousand talents of silver to the king's treasury for their destruction. The king said to Haman, "Do with them as it seemeth good to thee" (Esther 3:11).

Letters were sent to all the king's provinces to kill and destroy the Jews—young and old, women and children. Mordecai asked Queen Esther to go to the king and intervene. Esther replied that to go to the king without his prior invitation could amount to her losing her head. Mordecai made it clear to Queen Esther that if she did not act now, God would use another vessel to do the job and she and her father's house would be destroyed, "and who knoweth whether thou art come to the kingdom for such a time as this?" (Esther 4:14).

By Esther's request, all the Jews in the kingdom fasted for three days and thereafter she decided to go to the king and plead the case and if she perished, she perished. Meanwhile, Haman had made gallows ready to hang Mordecai thereon. He was boasting and rejoicing but all the Jews were in fear, tears and mourning. But through the influence of ONE PERSON, Esther, they were also in fasting and prayer.

The Bible reveals the power of prayer time and time again. May God revive a spirit of prayer in us in the season of any ambush planned against us. Amen!

Divine Intervention: The Restlessness of the King vs. the Honor of Mordecai

One night, the king could not sleep and he asked that the records of the chronicles be read to him. It was found out that Mordecai had saved his life from an assassination attempt by Bigthana and Teresh, and no honor had been done to Mordecai. At this same time, Haman was in the court to come to the king for Mordecai's head. At the king's command, Haman came in.

The king asked Haman, "What shall be done unto the man whom the king delighted to honor?" Haman thought it was for him and answered, "For the man who the king delighted to honor, let the royal apparel be brought which the king useth to wear, and the horse that the king rideth upon, and the crown royal which is set upon his head. And let this apparel and horse be delivered to the hand of one of the king's most noble princes, that they may array the man withal whom the king delighted to honor and bring him on horseback through the street of the city, and proclaim before him, thus shall it be done to the man whom the king delighted to honor" (Esther 6:7-9). Then the king said, "Do exactly as you have said without change and in haste to Mordecai, the Jew who sits at the king's gate."

Haman's pride and hatred turned him into a servant for the one who serves at the king's gate. Choose to serve the King of Kings and those who ride in high places of human pride will serve you at the command of the King of Kings. Hallelujah!

Divine Intervention: The Praying Queen vs. the Scheming Haman

Also, after the Jewish people's prayer and fasting, Esther had favor with the king, so she invited the king and Haman to a banquet. At the banquet, she revealed Haman's plans and pled for the Jews. So, Haman got hanged on the very gallows he had prepared for Mordecai. What an intervention?

So, How Many People Maintain the House?

First, God knows all things. He knows every evil intention of man, as well as those who seek Him. Haman sought to destroy the Jews and God had already prepared one vessel, in the person of Esther, for such a time as this. All the needed circumstances, including Mordecai and the contents of the Book of Chronicles, to deliver His people were in place and ready. And yes, God used only one to maintain the house. One who was yielded, selfless and seeking God to be used as His vessel, namely, Esther.

In that same way, I pray that we will receive double divine intentions in every situation we find ourselves in. I pray that any evil pursuit against us turns into the greatest testimony of our lifetime in Jesus' Name. Decide today, to be the "Esther" in the hand of God for someone else. Hallelujah!

E. An Impact Maker: Rahab, a Harlot

Rahab and the Two Spies

Following the death of Moses, at the beginning of Joshua's leadership, he sent two spies to scout out Jericho. The spies lodged with Rahab, the harlot. In Rahab's own words, *"I know that the LORD hath given you the land, and that your terror is fallen upon us, and all the inhabitants of the land faint because of you. For we have heard how the LORD dried up the water of the Red sea for you, when ye came out of Egypt; and what ye did unto the two kings of the Amorites, that were on the other side of Jordan, Sihon and Og, whom ye utterly destroyed"* (Joshua 2:9-10). She already knew what the Lord was capable of and was obviously in a place to be the one used by and for Him.

Rahab's Faith

Following Israel's departure from Egypt, God intentionally led them, not by the way of the Philistines which was shorter, but instead through the wilderness by the Red Sea, where God manifested His power by drowning the mighty Egyptian army (Exodus 14:13-31). Obviously, the knowledge of God's power had spread far and wide from Egypt to Jericho and beyond.

Second, Rahab mentioned the defeat of the Amorite kings. King Og of Bashan (Deuteronomy 31:4) was a man of great stature, like today's body builder, equivalent of Goliath in David's time. He ruled over sixty separate communities. King Og's defeat became proverbial because it dispelled any idea of invincibility based upon the king's appearance just like David and Goliath's situation.

The Amorite King Sihon on the other hand became famous as a result of his opposition to Israel on their way from Egypt to Israel. Under King Sihon's leadership, the Moabites were driven out and their territory became Sihon's (Deuteronomy 1:4-30).

At least, from the mouth of Rahab, these three mighty acts of God for Israel built her faith that there is a real God in Heaven. Not a god made by human hand, but the real Creator of the universe. Rahab believed in God and entrusted Him enough to put her life on the line to hide the Jewish spies.

Future of Rahab

As a result of trust in the Jewish God, Rahab, her parents and her brethren were protected and saved (Joshua 2:10-14). Also, according to Matthew's genealogy, Rahab is one of the four women mentioned in the family tree of the Son of God, Jesus. She was the great grandmother of King David (Ruth 4:18-21; Matthew 1:5). The Book of Hebrews acknowledges Rahab as a woman of faith (Hebrews 11:31).

God's Word tells us, *"For all have sinned, and come short of the glory of God"* (Romans 3:23). *"As it is written, There is none righteous, no, not one:"* (Romans 3:10). *"And as it is appointed unto men once to die, but after this the judgement"* (Hebrews 9:27). The question now is, is there hope for a prostitute bound for hell to totally trust in God and change her destiny? I believe Rahab's story shows us the answer is yes!

It took only one person, Rahab, to maintain the house and bring her entire family into the Kingdom of God, and even be in the family tree of the Lord Jesus Christ.

All these examples of impact-makers from different backgrounds, situations and circumstances give us the hope that none of us are useless to God if we will boldly yield our all to Him and say out loud to Him, "Here am I, send me."

All God needs to impact a nation, a generation, a family, a city, a church, a community, a company, a group, and on and on it goes, is ONE PERSON yielded to Him. Will you be that ONE PERSON?

CHAPTER THREE

THE NEEDED HEART QUALITIES

The Bible emphasizes the need to guard our hearts because out of it flows all the issues of life, according to Proverbs 4:23. This makes the heart very central to everything we want to do in life.

We know, for example, when the Word of God is sowed, depending on the condition of the heart, the seed of the Word will be fruitful or unfruitful. This doesn't mean the Word of God discriminates among people before it brings forth fruits. This can be cross referenced in Matthew 13.

This truth from the Word of God makes the type of heart a person has crucial to being able to make an impact the way God intends. So, I would like to highlight three virtues of the heart needed so the one person, chosen by God, can make the God-ordained impact wherever He places the person:

- A heart of integrity
- A willing heart
- A servant's heart

A. A Heart of Integrity

When talking about the qualities necessary for a Christian's heart, integrity is one quality that cannot be ignored, because it's the type of heart God desires and uses. It is written, *"And if thou wilt walk before me, as David walked, in integrity of heart, and in uprightness, to do according to all that I have commanded thee, and wilt keep my statutes and my judgements: Then I will establish the throne of thy kingdom upon Israel for ever, as I promised to David thy father, saying, There shall not fail thee a man upon the throne of Israel"* (1 Kings 9:4-5).

Integrity of heart means someone's words and actions are one. It means there is no difference between what they say and what they do. It takes a heart of integrity to admit mistakes and do what's necessary to make them right.

Psalm 78:72 (NIV) tells us, *"And David shepherded them with integrity of heart; with skillful hands he led them."* David was a man after God's own heart (Acts 13:22).

We know that God speaks truth and keeps His Word. Moses said in Numbers 23:19 (NKJV), *"God is not a man, that He should lie, Nor a son of man, that He should repent. Has He said, and will He not do? Or has He spoken, and will He not make it good?"*

An integrous heart is needed as much today as it's ever been. It is the centerpiece for a life to be used by God to do the extraordinary things that He desires.

Integrity is about being honest and fair with a strong sense of what is right and wrong. It's adhering to moral

and ethical principles, and goes to a person's character, that is, who they truly are. Integrity exemplifies who we are on the inside more than what we portray to others. Integrity is doing right when no one else is looking. Integrity involves keeping our word even when it hurts. Integrity of heart, therefore, is something that God is looking for in His people. He is pleased when we walk with integrity. It is written in Proverbs 11:20 (NLT), *"The LORD detests people with crooked hearts, but he delights in those with integrity."*

Job was such a man with a heart filled with integrity. He said, *"As long as my breath is in me, And the breath of God in my nostrils, My lips will not speak wickedness, Nor my tongue utter deceit…My righteousness I hold fast, and will not let it go; My heart shall not reproach me as long as I live"* (Job 27:3-6 NKJV).

In fact, not only is God pleased with such an integrous heart, but He also brags on it. The Bible tells us in 1 Chronicles 29:17 (NASB), *"Since I know, my God, that You put the heart to the test and delight in uprightness, I, in the integrity of my heart, have willingly offered all these things; so now with joy I have seen Your people, who are present here, make their offerings willingly to You."*

Integrity is not an optional quality needed by a person ready to be used by God for His glorious impact in this life, nation, generation, family, church, and/or workplace among others. It is a great key that sustains a person in the place of impact where God positions him or her.

Those who are ready to be used by God to "maintain the house" must commit to live a life of integrity. This honors God. So, decide to honor God with all your heart.

B. A Willing Heart

God decided to create man with free will so we can freely and decisively choose Him or reject Him. He didn't create man as a robot that He could manipulate. God created us in His image and gave us the ability to freely engage in a heart-to-heart relationship.

In our day and season, God still respects our free will and chooses a willing heart over a heart holding back from yielding freely to Him. Our willingness determines how much God can entrust into our hands and relate to us.

If we set our mind to achieve something and are willing to deal with whatever may come our way, nothing is impossible. There may be hurdles but the persuasion that everything is possible drives people to overcome challenges of all kinds. When God is the motivation and His Word is the driving passion that makes us willing, then God can take us to any height to make uncommon impact.

The word "willing" means cheerfully consenting. A readiness to be obedient, praying, studying the Word of God, and service all characterize the heart of the child of God.

God does the unbelievable things, not necessarily through the competent and qualified by worldly standards, but the ones with the willing hearts to serve God. Apostle Paul reminds us that God does not call the qualified, but He qualifies the called. All we need is a willing heart and availability. This implies that the deposition of your heart signals to God that you are willing to run the race He sets before you, no matter the risk or cost. Is your heart so full of many cares of this life that it is difficult for you to yield willingly to His direction and instruction for your life?

Remember, a willing heart is a great asset to becoming the one who maintains the house.

C. A Servant's Heart

"…but whoever wants to become prominent among you shall be your servant, and whoever desires to be first among you shall be your slave; just as the Son of Man did not come to be served, but to serve, and to give His life as a ransom for many" (Matthew 20:26-28 NASB).

A servant, according to Merriam Webster dictionary online, is one who serves others. Especially, the one who performs duties about the person or home of a master or personal employer.

The desire to serve God and others will drive doors open for the man led by God on a mission. We are each one person but every life counts and each one of us has a purpose here on Earth. God placed us here not to be rejected and dejected people subjected to purposelessness and fruitlessness in life. We are on God's agenda as individuals He can use for divine impact.

Satan will do anything to stop the one person God want to use but it will take our cooperating with the devil's deceits and lies for him to stop us. If we refuse and instead submit to God, He will bring His purpose to pass.

The decision to serve God as He directs our life demands a submissive heart. A servant's heart is to please their master. A servant committed to pleasing their master can be exalted by the master anytime. Our God is a just God and His key to true greatness demands serving from the heart.

The Bible says in Colossians 3:22-24 (NASB), *"Slaves, obey those who are your human masters in everything, not with eye-service, as people-pleasers, but with sincerity of heart, fearing the Lord. Whatever you do, do your work heartily, as for the Lord and not for people, knowing that it is from the Lord that you will receive the reward of the inheritance. It is the Lord Christ whom you serve."* A servant's heart is our key to divine promotions and upliftment in life. It is the sure foundation for divine inheritance issued by the Lord in our name.

Declare wholeheartedly that, "My Father is God. My leader is Christ. My teacher is the Holy Spirit." It is written in Matthew 23:8-12 (NKJV):

> *"But you, do not be called 'Rabbi'; for One is your Teacher, the Christ, and you are all brethren. Do not call anyone on earth your father; for One is your Father, He who is in heaven. And do not be called teachers; for One is your*

Teacher, the Christ. But he who is greatest among you shall be your servant. And whoever exalts himself will be humbled, and he who humbles himself will be exalted."

A servant's heart towards God and others requires:

- A submissive attitude.
- A humble inner resolve.
- A commitment to please God.
- A dedication to serve all men knowing it is being done for the Lord.

Decide to be the one person who God can use to maintain His house by allowing Him to work in your heart His integrity, His willingness of heart and the servant's Spirit needed. Hallelujah!

CHAPTER FOUR

WHAT IT TAKES TO
MAINTAIN THE HOUSE

A. Count the Cost!

Kwan Tzu, a Chinese Poet, once said: "If you are thinking a year ahead, sow seed. If you are thinking ten years ahead, plant a tree. If you are thinking a hundred years ahead, educate people. By sowing seed once, you will harvest once. By planting a tree, you will harvest tenfold. By educating people, you will harvest one hundredfold."[1]

In the cost of making a difference, one must always assess themselves by God's opinion, not man's opinion. People see us as we see ourselves. Age should never be a deterrent in making a difference. It is very vital and essential to consider only God's opinion and live it out.

Ponder on the following thoughts whilst counting the cost:

- We must be well-established in our Christ-identity. The cost of making a difference will demand

---

[1] Kwan Tzu, Chinese Poet, C. 500 B.C., retrieved on May 7, 2024, https://www.facebook.com/featherandfrond/photos/a.1773807989527479/1870740516500892/?type=3.

having a positive image. Such an image involves seeing ourselves through the eyes of God and through the truths in His living Word.

- Refuse comparisons with others. Anytime you compare yourself with others, you may become bitter, offended and unhappy. Compare yourself with God's plan for your life. The focus on God's purpose for your life makes fulfilling His plan achievable. You will be a duplicate if you try to be someone else so be the best that you can to make the difference.

- Be willing to start small. Every big thing starts small so do not despise small beginnings. To make a difference, agree with God that though the beginning is small, the latter end shall greatly increase (Job 8:7). Amen! God has promised to make us the head and not the tail. Small beginnings are of God and in counting the cost, small beginnings are opportunities for God to show forth His praise and glory as we maintain the house. Amen!

B. Obey God!

If we are in God's will, it makes the difference because He always orders our steps and stops when we are in obedience. The Word of God says, except the Lord builds the house, we labor in vain when we try to build it ourselves. To maintain the house, we must be obedient and in so doing, the Lord will perfect all that concerns us.

After every victory, there is a battle, but as we stay obedient to the Word of God, He will turn every mourning into dancing. He will turn all the impossibilities into possibilities.

A wise man once said, the difference between ordinary and extra ordinary is the word "extra." The biggest enemy of best is "good." So don't let how good we have been as a child of God stop us from yielding to what God has prepared ahead of us in life. Keep yielding to Him. Keep obeying and He will cause His shining light to spot us out among the lot for His glory. Hallelujah!

To be obedient to the Word of God as we maintain the house, we must:

- Grow in the Word.
- Establish a greater craving to study the Word.
- Enlarge our horizon in the Word.

Remember that the Word of God is profitable for teaching, reproving, correcting, and training in righteousness. His Word will make our lives profitable as we allow it to work in our lives. And yes, our feet will be placed on higher ground as we maintain the house in obedience to the Word of God.

C. Be Determined!

It takes determination for one person to maintain the house through the eyes of God. Determination requires making a firm decision about something. When God lays something on our hearts, we have to make a firm decision

to do that which God desires. We will never run out of provision pursuing the vision of the Great Provider. His vision comes from the light of the Word to help us see through every darkness and maintain the house in Jesus' name. Amen.

Indeed, the Word of God will be a lamp to our feet and a light to our path in maintaining the house. We will be wiser than our enemies as we hide the Word in our hearts. We will have stability during the storms of life as we determine to maintain the house. We will be matured and equipped to be ready for every good work through the Word of truth that sets us free. Amen!

D. Be Courageous!

What does it mean to be courageous? Courage is to be brave in the face of challenging circumstances. Courage is being able to take a risk with the knowledge of God's abiding presence. It takes courage to maintain the house.

Courage is to move forward without being deterred by the cost, emotional or spiritual pressures or discouragement through any other person. It is being scared to death but still saddling up. A courageous person will still act with confidence even in the face of fear. Because Abraham had that courage, he took the bold step to sacrifice Isaac.

To maintain the house:

- The secret is to focus on God and not circumstance. Take our eyes off circumstance and turn them toward our great defender and deliverer. David said in Psalm 121:1-2, *"I will lift up mine eyes unto the hills, from whence cometh my help. My help cometh from the LORD, which made heaven and earth."*
- Our strength for every task we face comes from God and His written Word. So, to develop courage, we need to mediate on God's Word. God's servant Job said, *"...I have treasured the words of His mouth More than my necessary food"* (Job 23:12 NKJV). The call to maintain the house involves great courage.
- We must learn to wait on God and be courageous.
- We will need to have strong faith in the Lord.
- We will have to set our priorities right. Our courage rests on God's assignment, upon the assurance of God's presence our focused determination, and the Word of God.

The outcome of showing courage is success. What holds us back from exercising courage is the baggage we still carry from the past. This allows fears, the enemy of faith, to persist. To maintain the house, we need to overcome fear and exercise courage to impact our generation. Amen!

E. Have Endurance!

It takes endurance to maintain the house. Everyone goes through challenges, but not everyone handles problems in a productive way. Job 27:21 says, *"The east wind carrieth him away, and he departeth: and as a storm hurleth him out of his place."* The east wind represents difficulty or adversity. We know, in the Bible, the Lord God caused the east wind to blow locusts into Egypt.

How do we handle storms? When we are in trouble, how do we react and respond? When we are under financial pressure, how do we react? How do we endure in the Lord?

God takes us to the wilderness to prepare us to die to self as we overcome the flesh. Unless the flesh is brought under subjection, the victory over sin will not last long. Once we know the purpose of our life, the seed that God has planted in our spirits, we have to let go and let everything that does not please God die. The seed must die with its flesh before it changes its form and becomes a plant. God deals with our flesh because no flesh shall glory in His presence.

David endured in the wilderness for several years before he became a king. Joseph was hidden in the prison though he was a prime minister in the making. David was in distress when the Amalekites invaded and took all the women and children captive and set their city on fire. In our walk with the Lord, as we maintain the house, we will reach a place where we think all is lost and the enemy has invaded us. But our reliable and dependable God is able to bring restoration, establish us, strengthen, and perfect all that concerns us through endurance. It is written in 1 Peter 5:10, *"But the God of all grace, who hath called us unto his eternal glory by Christ Jesus, after that ye have suffered a while, make you perfect, stablish, strengthen, settle you."* God will provide as we endure to maintain the house through His will.

F. Be Faithful!

God will sometimes entrust us with small responsibilities to see how we handle them. If we are faithful with the little He has given us to maintain, He will entrust us with more. If we are faithful in our own homes, God will entrust our community to us. It takes faithfulness to maintain the house.

Proverbs 20:6-7 says, *"Most men will proclaim every one his own goodness: but a faithful man who can find? The just man walketh in his integrity: his children are blessed after him."* To maintain the house, living godly lives with integrity as faithful individuals to God and His Word is very important. We should be living to obediently listen to God and no one else. A life full of love, joy, peace, longsuffering, and gentleness among others are part of the fruit of the Spirit that reflects a faithful person's life.

Chose to be God-controlled and not circumstances-controlled as a faithful person. Our greatness is the measure of our faithful surrender to obey His will. Be a faithful person who builds their home, encourages, appreciates, and lives peaceable with all people. Such a person is careful not to always rebuke or criticize others in public to shame them, doesn't judge and condemn people, does not flare up due to a negative response but rather gives room for other mistakes, forgives easily, and settles disputes quickly. A faithful person who maintains the house trusts in the Lord with all their heart. They do not lean on their own understanding. In all their ways, they acknowledge the Lord to direct their path and that of the family. So, choose today to be that faithful person God will use.

G. Commit to Prayer!

It takes commitment in prayer to maintain the house. Persistency in prayer pays off. The night Jesus was betrayed was a test of commitment for the disciples. Will they stay? Will they run away? Will they give up immediately? Will they continue in hope and faith? Things will happen in our lives that will make us feel and have a legitimate reason to quit, but we need to stick with it whether we feel like maintaining the house or not. Our flesh is too weak to keep any commitment, but the grace and mercy of God abounds to help us keep the commitments that we have made to maintain the house.

The Word of God in Mark 1:35 (NIV) says, *"Very early in the morning, while it was still dark, Jesus got up, left the house and went off to a solitary place, where he prayed."* Also, it is written in Matthew 14:20-23 (NIV), *"They all ate and were satisfied, and the disciples picked up twelve basketfuls of broken pieces that were left over. The number of those who ate was about five thousand men, besides women and children. Immediately Jesus made the disciples get into the boat and go on ahead of him to the other side, while he dismissed the crowd. After he had dismissed them, he went up on a mountainside by himself to pray…"* In Daniel 6:10 (NIV), the Word of God says, *"Now when Daniel learned that the decree had been published, he went home to his upstairs room where the windows opened toward Jerusalem. Three times a day he got down on his knees to prayed, giving thanks to his God, just as he had done before."*

Pray requires consistency and persistent commitment. Jesus taught that men ought to pray and not faint. He emphasized the need to pray without ceasing. To pray "without ceasing" implies:

- Constancy (Colossians 4:2)
- Perseverance (Romans 12:12; Ephesians 6:18; Luke 18:1)

"And he spake a parable unto them to this end, that men ought always to pray, and not to faint;" (Luke 18:1).

Final Thought:

Remember, all information discussed in this book is not easy to live out daily. The pillar that holds our life will grant us the grace to walk in them and fulfill them. Here are a few things you can do:

- Prayerful identify which "house" God wants to use you to maintain. Nothing can stop you if you are determined to maintain that house. Every effort you put in to maintain the house will be worthwhile. At the end of the day, your success in maintaining the house will bring you joy and will make you smile. You will forget all the pains and frustrations you incurred.

• Never forget to always seek God continuously and in each little step after the other. Take the advice of Proverbs 12:11,24, *"He that tilleth his land shall be satisfied with bread: but he that followeth vain persons is void of understanding…The hand of the diligent shall bear rule: but the slothful shall be under tribute."* Be diligent and consistent with God and the overflow of His outpoured blessings shall crown your life. God's school of success is that He blesses the hard work of the man who goes for it.

• Recall that it took one person to bring salvation. God will want to use you to introduce someone to this redemptive Word through our Lord Jesus Christ. Be always ready to be used by God for such a purpose. Certainly, know that God is able to do exceeding, abundantly above all that we think and ask (Ephesians 3:20).

• Also, the Word of God says in John 10:10 (NKJV), *"The thief does not come except to steal, and to kill, and to destroy. I have come that you may have life, and that you may have it more abundantly."* Don't let the thief steal the zeal to maintain the house. Receive by faith the abundant life the Lord Jesus has given you and walk in this daily. Decide to study and mediate on the Word so your ways will be prosperous and you will have good success (Joshua 1:8). So, as you work hard to maintain the house, God's blessings will be your portion to His glory. Amen!

All that God needs to impact a nation, a generation, a family, a city, a church, a community, a company, a group, and on and on it goes, is ONE PERSON yielded to Him. Will you be that ONE PERSON?

CHAPTER FIVE

SALVATION

The thought that God can and will use one person to advance His course is great. To know that God can use us to accomplish something extraordinary is even better. But, to have the revelation that God has freely provided what it takes for each person to be the one person He created them to be is unbelievably awesome.

That is exactly what it is. God has a purpose for creating us in His image. We are wonderfully and fearfully made. *"For You formed my inward parts; You covered me in my mother's womb. I will praise You, for I am fearfully and wonderfully made; Marvelous are Your works, And that my soul knows very well"* (Psalm 139:13-14 NKJV).

This truth should propel us to get to know the God who can take one life and make it glorious no matter all the earthly background and mistakes in a person's life. No baby born was an accident to God. A pregnancy might have been unplanned, but no child is without a God-designed purpose. *"For I know the thoughts that I think toward you, says the LORD, thoughts of peace and not of evil, to give you a future and a hope"* (Jeremiah 29:11 NKJV).

This means, God has a future for each life and that includes all of us. This future and expected end that God has for us is a provision of His grace. That means, His unmerited, unearned, undeserved, and unconditional favor has provided everything we need to be the one person that He has designed us to be. This is us becoming that person who maintains the house.

But the provisions God has made for our life can be fully accessed when we get to know the Provider and Creator of all things. When we get to know the One who formed us in our mother's womb for a glorious purpose, we discover our true purpose.

We will all agree that there can be no one to know a product on the market better than the creator of the product. He will also be in a better place to fix any problem with that product.

So, acknowledging that there is a Maker and this Maker formed us and placed us in this life for a purpose will start us on the journey of discovering who we really are. This will also help us appreciate the passion and love this Maker has for us. It is because of this love that God has for us and the whole world that He has provided the Lord Jesus Christ, His only begotten Son, to come and die for the sins of the world. The Bible tells us, *"For God so loved the world that He gave His only begotten Son, that whoever believes in Him should not perish but have everlasting life"* (John 3:16 NKJV).

This is the provision of His grace. *"For the grace of God that bringeth salvation hath appeared to all men"* (Titus 2:11). Accepting this provision of God's love by His grace is what reconciles a person back to God. This reconciliation to God is called Salvation.

The truths about salvation can be summarized and communicated as follows:

1. The love of God and His good plans for each person must be shared.
2. The sin of man separates him from God and His wonderful plans for our lives.
3. Jesus Christ is the only way to the Father. He gives us full access to the good plans and promises for God for us.
4. So, make the decision to receive Jesus Christ as Savior and Lord. This is the key to have the fulfilled life God has planned and prepared out of love for each person.

Have You Heard of the Four Spiritual Laws? a booklet by the late Dr. Bill Bright of Campus Crusade for Christ, is a recommended read to get more details and understanding of how to reach our world with the salvation message.

So, Salvation is a gift available by God's grace through faith for each person. Sin caused man to be separated from God. Man cannot, from his own effort, close the gap to God with good morals or good deeds of any form or kind. This means, how good and moral I am does not bring me the salvation that God gives.

- Romans 3:10 (NKJV) says, *"As it is written: 'There is none righteous, no, not one;'"*
- James 2:10 (NKJV) says, *"For whoever shall keep the whole law, and yet stumble in one point, he is guilty of all."* Why? Because each man has sinned. Yes, you and me too!
- Romans 3:23 (NKJV) says, *"for all have sinned and fall short of the glory of God."* So, no person can do anything to pay for all his or her sins.
- Romans 6:23 (NKJV) says, *"For the wages of sin is death..."* This is the wages that each man deserves. So, God required a perfect sacrifice to pay for the sins of this world and only Jesus could offer Himself for us.
- John 1:29 (NKJV) says, *"The next day John saw Jesus coming toward him and said, 'Behold! The Lamb of God who takes away the sin of the world!'"*

This is the great demonstration of God's love by grace to all mankind. Yes, the truth is that Jesus gave Himself in our place to pay for the sins He did not commit so that whoever believes in Him should not perish but have an everlasting life.

The Bible says:

"But God demonstrates His own love toward us, in that while we were still sinners, Christ died for us" (Romans 5:8 NASB).

"…Christ died for our sins according to the Scriptures, and that He was buried, and that He was raised on the third day according to the Scriptures," (1 Corinthians 15:3-4 NASB).

"For God so loved the world that He gave His only begotten Son, that whoever believes in Him should not perish but have everlasting life" (John 3:16 NKJV).

This is precious. Everyone who is ready to discover the great purpose of God for their life should continue discovering the wonders of God in every situation and freely receive this gracious gift of salvation through faith in Jesus Christ. Salvation brings us eternal life.

The Bible teaches us how to receive this precious gift of salvation if you haven't already. It is written in Romans 10:8-10 (NIV), *"But what does it say? 'The word is near you; it is in your mouth and in your heart,' that is, the message concerning faith that we proclaim: If you declare with your mouth, 'Jesus is Lord,' and believe in your heart that God raised him from the dead, you will be saved. For it is with your heart that you believe and are justified, and it is with your mouth that you profess your faith and are saved."*

Receiving salvation is believing in your heart that through Jesus' death on the cross, all your sins have already been paid for and so you receive the forgiveness He offers. By believing that in your heart, He declares your sins are forgiven. That is justification through Jesus Christ. He washes you clean and it is just as if you have

never sinned. Hallelujah! This all takes place within you as you believe in your heart.

Then you confess with your mouth, "Jesus is Lord." This means that you acknowledge and profess that He has absolute Lordship in your life as your savoir. You turn your life over to Him so He can defend you when the accuser of the brethren, the devil, shows up with your sins to condemn and accuse you of anything. He, Jesus, can step in and defend and declare you free by showing the evidence of His nail-pierced hands, His pierced side and all His stripes, that He has paid the price for every sin on your behalf. Hallelujah! This one gift is the most important in all your life on Earth and it is the key to accessing the relationship with God and all the riches of His grace.

Jesus offers us an intimate relationship with Him and His Father, God. This is the very definition of the eternal life He gives us freely at salvation. This precious life is also referred to as abundant life because through this eternal relationship between mortals and immortal God flows the true nature of God into our lives. This is having life in full.

"Now this is eternal life: that they know you, the only true God, and Jesus Christ, whom you have sent" (John 17:3 NIV).

"The thief comes only to steal and kill and destroy; I have come that they may have life, and have it to the full" (John 10:10 NIV).

Being unsaved is equivalent to a person who's drowning and is in desperate need of help which they're not able to provide themselves. Jesus came to the Earth to offer us a hand, to pull us from the darkness, to save us. And then to offer us a new life that is free from the power and influence of the darkness that was drowning us.

> *"For he has rescued us from the dominion of darkness and brought us into the kingdom of the Son he loves, in whom we have redemption, the forgiveness of sins"* (Colossians 1:13-14 NIV).

Also, beyond the grave, the Christian has the promise of a crown of righteousness, citizenship in the everlasting Kingdom and the assurance that the Lamb of God will lead us beside still waters and wipe away all our tears. These truths should motivate each person to receive, by faith, this gracious offer of God's love for us.

Pray and Be Saved!

Decide today to speak this confession to make Jesus Lord of your life:

"Dear Jesus, I accept that I am a sinner and in need of a savior. I accept You as the one who came on Earth, died for my sins and resurrected again. I confess You as the Lord of my life and I believe that I am justified right now by Your cleansing

blood. Thank You, Jesus, that I am now saved and have become the child of God. Amen!"

God is not requiring you to do anything for Him. God rather has offered you a new life full of adventures and experiences of the life of His righteousness at work in you and through you from today until eternity.

> *"Therefore, if anyone is in Christ, the new creation has come: The old has gone, the new is here!"* (2 Corinthians 5:17 NIV).

> *"God made him who had no sin to be sin for us, so that in him we might become the righteousness of God"* (2 Corinthians 5:21 NIV).

Decide today to live this life with God well. After you have prayed and gotten saved, you need to be discipled so you can grow in your relationship with God. This will start having a positive impact in your relationship with others. This is because the transformation of your life after being saved happens through the renewing of your mind.

Live for Jesus

I encourage you to practice these:

1. Read the Bible daily!
   a. *"as newborn babes, desire the pure milk of the word, that you may grow thereby,"* (1 Peter 2:2 NKJV).

b. Reading the Word and pondering on what you read through the day will help you keep the Word active on your mind. The result is renewing your mind and becoming transformed.

c. Some use the Bible as an acronym to mean:
- **B**eliever's
- **I**nstructions
- **B**efore
- **L**eaving the
- **E**arth

So, spend time in this Living Word to discover the instructions about life that will cause you to be ready to be the person God uses to maintain the house. Hallelujah!

2. Spend time in prayer daily!

a. Prayer is communication with God. It is not just speaking but also making time to listen to what God has on His heart. This deepens the relationship with God and helps you to know His voice so that you can follow Him daily.

b. *"Then Jesus told his disciples a parable to show them that they should always pray and not give up"* (Luke 18:1 NIV).

3. Practice the truths from the Word daily!

a. Practice Love: *"And you shall love the LORD your God with all your heart, with all your soul, and with all your mind, and with all your strength.' This is the first commandment. And the second, like it, is this:*

'You shall love your neighbor as yourself.' There is no other commandment greater than these" (Mark 12:30-31 NKJV).

b. Live by Faith: *"And without faith it is impossible to please God, because anyone who comes to him must believe that he exists and that he rewards those who earnestly seek him"* (Hebrews 11:6 NIV).

c. Put on Righteous: *"and to put on the new self, created to be like God in true righteousness and holiness"* (Ephesians 4:24 NIV).

4. Watch your tongue daily!

a. With your own words, you can create room for sin and Satan to keep influencing your life, even though you are a child of God or you agree with the truths of God's Word. Start experiencing how the living power of scriptures change your life.

b. *"The tongue has the power of life and death, and those who love it will eat its fruit"* (Proverbs 18:21 NIV).

c. *"What man is he that desireth life, and loveth many days, that he may see good? Keep thy tongue from evil, and thy lips from speaking guile. Depart from evil, and do good; seek peace, and pursue it"* (Psalm 34:12-14).

d. *"...But those things which proceed out of the mouth come from the heart, and they defile a man. For out of the heart proceed evil thoughts, murders, adulteries, fornications, thefts, false witness, blasphemies..."* (Matthew 15:11,18-20 NKJV).

e. *"Do not let any unwholesome talk come out of your mouths, but only what is helpful for building others up according to their needs, that it may benefit those who listen"* (Ephesians 4:29 NIV).

Believe and Live the Life of Possibilities in God

Faith is a universal currency, and it pays and produces the same result on every part of the globe. It takes your believing in God to receive and enjoy His blessings. So, revelation is the determining factor in the world of the miraculous. Once you can see through your spiritual eyes, you are on a flight into the world of the supernatural. If you see possibilities, that is what will come to you.

- For the impossible to be possible, you have to be bold enough to say, "Because I trust in the Lord, I shall be as mount Zion which cannot be removed but abide forever."
- For the impossible to be possible, you must believe that the name of the Lord is a strong tower, the righteous run into it and is safe.
- For the impossible to be possible, you must believe the assurance of God in Luke 1:74-75 (NIV) where the Lord has promised *"to rescue us from the hand of our enemies, and to enable us to serve him without fear in holiness and righteousness before him all our days."*
- With Him all things are possible and cannot fail—not some things but **ALL** things are possible.

You must lean upon the Lord and trust God. Make sure He is in control of every situation because He is your Supreme source.

Don't allow negative thoughts to control and influence you. Refuse to dwell on negative thoughts, if you really want to see what might seem impossible manifest in your life.

God's inability to fail is based upon His unchanging character. He neither slumbers nor sleeps. He will not allow problems to crush you. He will not allow trials to overwhelm you if you believe that He will make the impossibilities possible. Your situation or challenge might seem or sound impossible, but you serve a living God who makes all things, situation and circumstances possible.

Get Water Baptized (Immersed in Water)

The death, burial and resurrection of Jesus for your sin are the facts of the Gospel. To be baptized is to be buried with Jesus in baptism, wherein also you are raised with Jesus through the faith of the operation of God who has raised Jesus from the dead (Colossians 2:12). If a person has not been immersed in water with the proper understanding of its significance (Romans 6:17), he/she has not been baptized scripturally and needs to go back under the water again.

Baptism washes away your sins by the blood of Jesus. Baptism brings you into Christ as said in Acts 2:38, *"Then Peter said unto them, Repent, and be baptized every one of you in*

the name of Jesus Christ for the remission of sins, and ye shall receive the gift of the Holy Ghost."

All that God needs to impact a nation, a generation, a family, a city, a church, a community, a company, a group, and on and on it goes, is ONE PERSON yielded to Him. Will you be that ONE PERSON?

ABOUT THE AUTHOR

 Currently based in Bolingbrook, Illinois, Deaconess Angeline Eshun Kesse, aka Mama Angie, is a dynamic woman of God with a burning passion to see God's Kingdom established on Earth as the presence of God fills all spheres of life. Her passion is getting the Lord's people ready for Heaven. Her spiritual destiny, teachings and counseling brings restoration and renews the mind for Christ.

Mama Angie, by divine grace, has a teaching, praying and counseling call from the Lord. She loves nurturing, training and grooming people for the Lord.

Delivering a down to Earth explanation of the Word of God, full of power and anointing, characterizes her ministry. Focusing on bringing Christ to others, they get empowered and healed as they are ministered to. Driven by the desire to see God's children rise to fulfill their divine assignments and heavenly callings, she emphasizes God's presence filling the earth.

She has spent over thirty years shepherding the children of God. She is the leader and founder of Bethel

Prayer Fellowship USA Inc: A Place of Spiritual Empowerment and Solutions.

She has five wonderful daughters, seven grandchildren, has been blessed with several spiritual sons, daughters and grandchildren, and has adopted and nurtured many others.

May God empower readers, through the keys in this book, to end all forms of human traditions and establish a Christlike mindset to make a difference.

We would love to hear from you. Share your story about how this book has changed your perspective and touched your life or send us your prayer request:

First Name:_____

Last Name:_____

Address:_____

City:_____

State:_____

Zip Code:_____

Country:_____

Testimony or Prayer Request:

_____

_____

_____

_____

_____

_____

_____

_____

_____

_____

Please fill the form and mail to:

Bethel Prayer Fellowship USA Inc:
354 Gehrig Circle
Bolingbrook, Illinois 60440
USA

Fellowship Email:
Bethelprayerfellowship05@gmail.com

Live on Zoom:
Meeting ID: 267 642 4403# (Passcode: 2020)

Audio Dial-In:
1-312-626-6799 US (Chicago)
1-646-558-8656 (US)
1-646-931-3860 (US)
1-929-205-6099 (US)-NY

Service Days and Chicago Times:
- Midnight Prayers: 12:30 a.m. to 2:00 a.m. (Monday thru Thursday)
- Morning Prayers: 10:00 a.m. to 12:30 p.m. (Monday thru Friday)
- All-Night Prayers: 11:00 p.m. to 3:30 a.m. (Fridays)
- Evening Prayers: 8:00 p.m. to 10:30 p.m. (Saturday and Sunday)

How many people maintain the house? All God needs to impact a nation, a generation, a family, a city, a church,

a community, a company, a group, and on and on it goes, is ONE PERSON yielded to Him. Will you be that ONE PERSON?

www.ingramcontent.com/pod-product-compliance
Lightning Source LLC
Chambersburg PA
CBHW071108120626
46546CB00003B/1302